THE

COUNCIL OF DOGS.

———

ILLUSTRATED WITH SUITABLE ENGRAVINGS.

———

LONDON:

PRINTED FOR J. HARRIS, SUCCESSOR TO E. NEWBERY, AT THE
ORIGINAL JUVENILE LIBRARY, THE CORNER OF
ST. PAUL'S CHURCH-YARD,

———

1808.

THE

COUNCIL OF DOGS.

———————

WHY a COUNCIL of DOGS was convened on the Plain,
The PRESIDENT SHEEP DOG thus rose to explain.—
   " This meeting I call, to complain of misusage
" From the poets, who now a days have a strange usage
" Of leading up Insects and birds to Parnassus,
' While, without rhyme or reason, unnotic'd they pass us.—
" Declare then those talents by which we may claim
" Some pretensions, I hope, to poetical fame.—
" *I* boast of whole legions, my voice who obey;
" Without me the Sheep, e'en the Shepherd, might stray—
" But no more of myself—Let each Dog of spirit,
" Stand forward and modestly state his own merit.
" But I charge you be gentle, let's hear of no growling,
" No grinning, no snarling, no snapping, no howling."

The GREYHOUND first rose, with a spring from his seat,
Scarcely bending the grass, that grew under his feet ;
His figure was airy, and placid his mien ;
Yet to flash in his eye indignation was seen.——
" Brave companions," said he, " shall *we* noble beasts
" Hear of *Butterflies Balls* and *Grasshoppers Feasts* ?
" Hear dinned in our ears, wherever we roam,
" The *Mask seeing Lion* and *Peacock at Home* ?
" Shall we hear all this, nor assert the fair fame
" That for ages long past has distinguished our name ?——
" Forbid it ye Dogs !——here behold me stand forth,
" To proclaim to the world my deserts, and my worth !——
" Keen and swift in the chace, I can boldly declare
" From my speed, as I follow, in vain flies the Hare ;
" Nay, while like the wind, I bound over the course
" My master comes lagging behind on his Horse.
" 'Twixt friends, I could laugh, at beholding the fuss
," And boasting men make of success due to us ,
" The truth is so obvious 'tis scarce worth enforcing ,
" Without our assistance they could not go coursing
" All you say," quoth the HARRIER, " dear coz, is most true,
" Yet I think it but just, to give each Dog his due ;

" So don't be offended if *I* dare disclose

" That *you* are not gifted,' like me, with a nose."

When the POODLE heard this, he laugh'd out aloud,

And all the Curs grinned, who were mixed in the crowd :

Then the Hound and the Grey-hound both flew at the Poodle

And called him a curl-coated Cur, and a noodle—

Poor Poodle was frighten'd at what he had done,

But being himself much addicted to fun,

And having no notion of running by scent,

He could not conceive the Hound seriously meant

To say, that the Grey-hound had no nose at all,

When he'd one twice as long as his own, tho' 'twas small.

" Come have done with your jaw," said the FOX HOUND in spleen,

" For how should a foreigner know what you mean ?

" May-hap he can dance, and I'm sure he can beg ;

" Let him run me a race, and I'll tye up a leg ;

" But in hunting, in truth, the HARRIER and BEAGLE,

" No more equal us, than the Hawk does the Eagle ;

" Trotting after a Hare is mere childish play,

" It may now and then serve, to kill a dull day.

" But *we*, at sun rise, seek the Fox in the cover,

" Drive him often before us, ten counties half over ;

" Sweep wild o'er the hill, or close at his brush

" Unchecked thro' the gorse, and the river we rush,

" And Phœbus once more must sink down to his nest,

" E'er we slacken our chace, or betake us to rest;

" So tempting our sport, Men think it atones

" For the maiming of limbs and the breaking of bones."

Said the STAG-HOUND—" All rivalships here I disclaim,

" Since for strength, and for speed, so well known is my fame,

" That I justly am reckon'd the first amongst hounds

" Yet our chace like the FOX-HOUNDS, with danger abounds,

" Nay, is sometimes attended with fatal effects,

" As in hunting of Stags, men *have* broken their necks."

" Oh þray say no more," said a poor MEAGRE CUR,

" It grieves me to think men such dangers incur;

" To mankind, I'm a friend of the genuine breed,

" A friend little known, but in th' hour of need;

" By this string round my neck I guide my poor master,

" And true to his touch, I go slower or faster;

" Oh Pity his sorrows, for he is stone blind,

" And without my assistance his way could not find;

" But I lead him with caution through Alleys and Streets,

" And rejoice to observe the relief that he meets:

' And when to our lodging at night we repair,

" Of the food he's collected, he gives me a share."

Then a SPANIEL advanced, with a courtier-like mien,

His manners were gentle, his coat soft, and clean,

His nose was jet black, and his ears were so long,

They swept on the ground, as he passed through the throng,

Thus he spoke—

" We boast to mankind an attachment so pure,

" That docile, and patient, their blows we endure :

" We can hunt, we can quest, and what's more we can trace

" A descent long ennobled by favour and grace ;

" For our ancestors portraits are still to be seen

" With those of the *Babes* of *King Charles* and his *Queen*

" You boast of your rank, Sir," the WATER-DOG cried

As he shook his rough coat, that was scarcely yet dried,

" But in sport who with me can compare?—have you seen,

" Where the bush-fringed pool is mantled with green,

" How I wind, thro' the reeds and the rushes, my way,

" And the haunt of the Snipe, or the Mallard betray ?

" How, when loud sounds the Gun, aroused by the crash

" (As the fall of the victim, is marked by the splash)

" Leaping forward I bear off the prey at a dash ?"

8

" Tis enough—you have merit—but I think it better

" To mention my claims," quoth the feather-tailed SETTER.

" The dew of the morn I with rapture inhale,

" When check'd in my course, by the scent breathing gale, ʒ

" In caution low crouching each gesture displays,

" Where the covey lies basking, or sportively plays;

" My net bearing master I watch as I creep,

" Till encircled, the brood is enthralled at a sweep."

The POINTER then rose, and observ'd—"Sir, your trade is

" So gentle and quiet, it might suit the ladies,

" Poor things who would scream at the sound of a gun,

" Which we POINTERS consider as part of the fun.

" We range the wide fallows, or quarter the stubble,

" While the labouring sportsman, alive to each double,

" Hails the high stiffen'd tail, and the motionless joint,

" And cautiously warns the whole field of the point;

" As by magic transfixt, all the signal obey—

" With the death dealing tube, he hastes up to his prey."

To the Pointer a bandy leg'd TURNSPIT replied,

" All you've said, worthy kinsman, cannot be denied,

" As to pastimes and sports—but allow me to say

" I to men some good turns have done in my day.

" When the sportsman returns to his meal, what avail

" Your ranging, and pointing, and high stiffen'd tail?

" Of your posture so graceful, good Sir, you may boast it;

* " *A quoi bon* your game, if *I* did not roast it?"

A bristly Scotch TERRIER, his eyes black and keen,

Thus attack'd the last speaker—" Pray what do you mean?

" To boast of your service no longer of use;

" If you still roasted meat, there *might* be some excuse;

" But Smoak-jacks, and Rumfords, and other new hits

" Ease you (thank the Dog Star) from turning of spits.

" But to be in such haste to record your own worth,

" And speak before me, a famed dog of the North,

" Who all vermine destroy, Mouse, Weazle, or Rat!"

Says the Turnspit—" why so can my mistress's Cat."—

" You crooked leg'd Cur," said the TERRIER, " to dare

" Such talents as mine, with a Cat's to compare "—

The PRESIDENT SHEEP-DOG to order now call'd 'em,

('Twas well they grew quiet, or else he'd have maul'd 'em)

He threaten'd the meeting should instantly close—

Here the PUG and the SPANIARD, each turn'd up his nose.

* N. B. This Dog was bred under a French Cook.

But a dappe BARBET, so blithe and so smart,
With his ruffles, and ruff, all shorn with such art,
Tript forward, and said his tricks he would play—
He tumbled,—fetch'd ball,—and down for dead lay,—
Then started alive to defend GEORGE THE THIRD,
While, in pleasure loud barking, their plaudits were heard.

EIGHT CURS, thus encouraged, stepp'd out with delight,
And suddenly rear'd on their hind legs upright,
They bow'd, and they curtsey'd with infinite skill,
And danced on the turf a graceful quadrille.

More MONGRELS rush forward, all eager to tell,
How their masters they serve, and in what they excel;
Each follow'd or Pedlar, or Tinker, or Gipsy,
And watch'd o'er the goods, while their masters got tipsy.

The POACHER'S-DOG trembling, and all in a fright,
Then whisper'd, *he* follow'd his master by night;
He never gave tongue, he safely could say,
And not telling tales, slunk slyly away.

" Stop a moment, dear Sir, and look not so rueful,
" But hearken to me who'm the Dog for a Truffle;
" Though your body be thin, and your spirits be low,
" Comparisons often will comfort bestow;

" Look at me, and acknowledge, that I'm somewhat leaner,
" For they famish poor TRUFFLER to make him the keener."
    At length rose the MASTIFF so gruff, and so surly,
That the Curs scamper'd off in a sad hurly burly.
" I am glad to observe that none of you dare
" To boast of your courage ; for, said he, to compare
" Your valour w th mine, in vain would you strive all,
" My Cousin the BULL-DOG alone is my rival ;
" We're both so undaunted, determined, and bold,
" That on what we have fasten'd, we never quit hold.
" He regrets that this meeting he cannot attend,
" But he's gone into Norfolk to visit a friend,
" And has left it with me his excuses to make,
" While *he* is engaged with the Bull at the stake.
    " Hold hold,"—cried a Dog of gigantic dimensions,
Who came from Hibernia to urge his pretensions,
" Of your valour so matchless you're wondrously full,
" But my homies you know, I'm the dog for a Bull ;
" And learn, my Progenitors, fam'd dogs of yore,
" Could do more in two days, than you in a score.
" Their brave feats I am told, are recorded by sages,
(Who wrote both of beasts and of men in past ages,)

" That the WOLF-DOGS of ERIN, so fierce in their rage,
" Dared in war with the Lords of the Forest engage,
" And could I but meet with the beasts they have slain,
" I'm the dog, my dear joy, to kill them again."
Cried the MASTIFF in haste, as he rose to reply,
" Your merit, dread Sir, I don't mean to deny,
" For historical facts I'm inclined to rely on,
" And tis said that your Ancestors vanquished the Lion ;
" Allowed—But I'm told, that at *present* your race
* " In Kamstchatka but fills a subordinate place.
  Here a great dog observ'd—" Don't think me romantic,
" Yet my Parents were born beyond the Atlantic ;
" But to brag of descent is not in my plan ;
" For merit more sterling I'm valu'd by man :
" Through the journey of life, I his footsteps attend,
" By night I'm his guardian, by day I'm his friend ;
" My pastime's to dive in the River or Sea,
" For the rage of the deep has no terrors for me ;
" Nor for pleasure alone these risks do I brave,
" Kind fortune allowed me, my master to save,
" When, expiring, he struggled in vain with the wave."

* Vide Buffon—Article Dogs.

Said the PRESIDENT " Sir—I admire your skill,

" But I hear you're disposed your own mutton to kill;

" If true this report, don't think me too bold,

" In advi-ing you not to chuse Sheep from my fold."

The LEARNED-DOG next—"I boast not of my learning,

" Though perhaps it has made me, than you more discerning ;

" I conceive you have none of you knowledge in Greek,

" Sufficient of ancient Dogs' merits to speak—

" I shall mention a few—The first of them this is,

" Poor ARGUS, the Dog of the wandering Ulysses ;

" He lived, the return of his master to greet,

" Then bounding for joy, fell dead at his feet.—

" I doubt if you've heard Alcibiades name,

" A Grecian fine gentleman, who, to his shame,

" To give the Athenians a subject to rail,

" Deprived a most beautiful Dog of his tail."*

When the Council heard this, the great members growl'd,

And every little Dog pitiously howl'd.

The clamour subsided—The wise Dog again,

Resumed his harangue, in a tedious strain ;—

* Vide Plutarch's Life of Alcibiades.

Spoke of Theseus's hounds, of the true Spartan breed ;—
And the hounds of Actæon, so famed for their speed—
Of three-headed Cerbérus, Guardian of Hell,
Whom Orpheus subdued with his musical spell.
How Hecuba changed, seeing dead Polydore,
And became—Vide Ovid—(here he heard the Dogs snore)
" Your patience my friends, I no longer will tire,
" But brief make excuses, at the earnest desire
" Of those friends from abroad, who all much lamented
" That chance or engagements their attendance prevented.
" The AFRICAN-DOG, said, that he did not dare
" Quit the warm coast of Guinea in clothing so spare ;
" The LAPLAND and DANE-DOG the gay POMERANIAN,
" The slender ITALIAN, sagacious SIBERIAN,
" All pleaded the times ; some could not get passports,
" Some feared BONAPARTE, some were stopt by their own courts,
" Some were mangy, distemper'd, and others insane,
" With a few ladies LAP-DOGS afraid of the rain."
He spake—On the sudden a howling went round
From each TERRIER and MASTIFF and POINTER and HOUND,
For, full in the midst of the council, a CUR
(Whose presence no member had noticed before)

Uprose to address them; blood-red was his eye,
His carcase was fleshless, and shrill was his cry,
His knees were all bent, as with weakness he shook,
And death and starvation scowled in his look.—
" You may talk of Parnassus and Poets," he cried,
" Of their scorn, and neglect, may complain in your pride,
" But that is all vanity, folly, conceit,
" The disgust of the pamper'd, the pride of the great;
" Look at me; I am starved—In yon hamlet I dwelt
" And contented for years no distresses I felt,
" Till the TAX, that my master had no means to pay,
" From the comforts of home drove me famished away;
" 'Tis for *life* I contend—Praise, Honour, Renown,
" The song of the Bard, or the laureate Crown,
" Will ne'er teach my blood in its freshness to flow,
" Ne'er teach me with health and with vigour to glow;
" Revenge, then, Revenge"————Exhausted he sunk,—
And back from the sight in horror they shrunk.
    " A silence ensued—Thus the president spoke,
" This Council, my friends, I wished to convoke
" Our rights to assert, but though each dog pretends
" To valour, or beauty, or skill, yet my friends
" If we look for success, much on union depends;

" Let no separate claims then this union betray,

" For remember the promise, *each dog has his day.*—

" Tis our aggregate worth must our merits decide,

" Our patience, sagacity, faithfulness tried ;

" We then shall deserve, if we don't obtain fame,

" And the Poets, not we, incur the just blame ;

" This perhaps too may cause our arch-foe to relent,

" And move to compassion the hard hearted D * * * ;

" If so, my companions, the good that may follow,

" Is better than all we can get from APOLLO."

The PRESIDENT spoke, the fair omen they hail,

And in sign of delight each dog wagged his tail.

Thus agreed, e'er they rose, their thanks were resolved

Nem : Con : to the chair, and the meeting dissolved.

THE END.

H. Bryer, Printer, Bridge-Street, Blackfriars.

CPSIA information can be obtained
at www.ICGtesting.com
Printed in the USA
BVHW090535070722
641462BV00001B/154